赤内接
INSCRIBED RED

準えるの俳句バージョン芥川
Haiku Versions After Akutagawa Ryūnosuke

ERIC HOFFMAN

SPUYTEN DUYVIL
New York City

ISBN 978-1-959556-97-8

Library of Congress Control Number: 2024930927

FOREWORD: ABOUT AKUTAGAWA

I have no conscience at all—least of all an artistic
conscience. All I have is nerves.
>   Akutagawa Ryūnosuke,
>   "Spinning Gears," tr. Jay Rubin

B est known in both Japan and the West as the
author of "In a Grove," a gnomic meditation
on the mercurial nature of human perception and
the inspiration for Kurosawa Akira's brilliant film
Rashōmon—the film that introduced Japanese
cinema to world audiences—Akutagawa Ryūnosuke
(1 March 1892 – 24 July 1927) is among the most
important authors in modern, post-Meiji Japan. His
brief yet captivating and influential career spanned
only a few decades, primarily during the interwar
Taishō era (1912-1926), a period of comparative
liberalism and decadence amid two phases of
external imperialist expansionism and aggression
and internal repression. Yet in that time he managed
to author a number of the most highly regarded

works in Japanese literature: the aforementioned "In a Grove," "Rashōmon" (on which Kurosawa's film draws only its partial setting and evocative title), "The Nose," "Hell Screen," and "Spinning Gears," to name a few. Unique among Japanese authors, nearly all of his short stories have been widely translated, largely due to the quality of his writing—namely his narrative sophistication and psychological insight—as well as the universality of his themes.

At the time Akutagawa wrote–during the first three decades of the 20th century—the forms of narrative fiction most popular in Japan were examples of modernist realism: the "I-novel" and proletarian literature, each influenced by Japan's exposure to the West when in 1868 Japan formally re-opened to the outside world following nearly 200 years of almost complete isolation. In that time, the Western world had been fundamentally changed by the Industrial Revolution, and the Japanese, in the interest of self-preservation, quickly acknowledged the need to catch up. This transformation of Japanese society was already rapidly underway in the year of

Akutagawa's birth (in the hour, day, month, and year of the dragon; his given name means "dragon born") and all but completed by the year of his death (1927) by suicide at the age of 35 (or 36 by the Japanese count).

Both the "I-novel" and the proletariat forms presented severe limitations against which Akutagawa reacted: the former tended to be narcissistic, exhibitionist, and nihilistic, and the latter idealistically concerned with the diagnoses of society's class-based ills. Deeply knowledgable of Eastern and Western literature, Akutagawa took full advantage of the decadence of the Taishō era and the dispiritedness similar to that of fin de siècle Europe, of "art for art's sake." Akutagawa's solution, then, was elegant in its simplicity: his fiction, almost exclusively in the short form, is intentionally artificial, aphoristic, and spare, draws its themes and settings from the deep wellspring of medieval Japanese history and folklore—subjects his contemporaries, in their eagerness to embrace Western aesthetics were all-too willing to discard—and interprets them through a distinctly contemporary, psychologically complex lens. His strategy complements a post-Meiji Japanese psyche still haunted by pre-Meiji archetypes. This rich tapestry provided Akutagawa with a sufficient canvas with which to stage his intense, nerve-wracking dramas of human passion, confusion, and desperation. Perhaps sensing that he had ironically self-imposed too severe a restriction in retaliation against external restrictions, toward the end of his life his work veered towards autobiography, non-fiction, and satire, yet it never lost its razor-sharp focus and its nakedly metaphysical edge.

As celebrated as Akutagawa is as a short story writer, his haiku—the first of which was composed in 1906, the same year Akutagawa began to read contemporary Japanese literature, written under the *haigo* of "Gaki," a reference to a hungry demon as depicted in a medieval Japanese Buddhist painting of hell—is relatively unknown outside of Japan, and rarely translated. This oversight might be due to the relative difficulties Akutagawa's haiku presents to a translator, principally his frequent, intentionally archaic use of classical Japanese and Chinese references. Moreover, for all of their linguistic sophistication, the poems themselves remain unrepentantly classical in form, adhering to well-defined literary conventions already well-established by the 16th century: the 5-7-5 *on* structure, the season word (*kigo*), the requirement for overt or implied reference to a specific season, and cutting word (*kireji*), often used in the middle of a haiku, to separate the haiku into two contrasting independent thoughts or images.

Contemporary with Akutagawa, haiku was undergoing a metamorphosis that rivaled other art forms in the wake of Japan's belated encounter with innovations in Western literary forms. Under the leadership of Masaoka Shiki (1867-1902)—who coined the term "haiku"—the form was rescued from the very conventions that threatened to render it obsolete in the face of these momentous transformations of modern Japanese society. For Shiki, the haiku, long practiced by hobbyists through a steadfast adherence to strict rules, could be revitalized only through realistic depictions of nature as actually observed—a practice Shiki named *shisei* or "sketch from nature"—as opposed to formulaic depictions of nature derived from literary tradition. A rift occurred when Shiki's primary acolytes, Takahama Kyoshi (1874-1959) and Kawahigashi Hekigotō (1873-1937), took haiku into two radically different directions: Kyoshi retained the season word and 5-7-5 structure so integral to Shiki—after Shiki's death, Kyoshi took over editorship from Shiki of the key haiku journal *Hototogisu*—while Hekigotō preserved the kigo yet abandoned the 5-7-5, resulting in an essentially free verse haiku, a move further radicalized by Hekigotō's follower Ogiwara Seisensui (1884-1976) and his development of the *Jiyuritsu* haiku, which fully dispensed of the kigo.

By comparison, Akutagawa's haiku, like his fiction, deeply influenced by the haiku of his peer, the celebrated novelist Natsume Sōseki (1867-1916), eschews modernism in its embrace of classical forms; Akutagawa's haiku derive as much from literary tradition as from lived experience. If not for their precision, learning, and psychological depth, his haiku, at least on the surface, often share more in common with the *haikai* of the 17th and 18th century than with 20th century haiku as practiced by Shiki and his followers. These haiku are as much shisei as they are homages to a hundreds of years old classical tradition. Frequently they portray a modern consciousness in relationship with an idealized nature that exists more within the Japanese psyche than the landscape that surrounds him.

Nevertheless, present in both Akutagawa's fiction and haiku is the tension of transformation, in which much of the drama lies in Akutagawa's exploration of the timeless foundations of the natural world in search of the handholds and footholds needed to traverse the unforgivably treacherous and ever-shifting landscape of the human spirit undergoing a profound yet ultimately mysterious metamorphosis, the contours and features of which have yet to be fully understood.

Translator's Note

The haiku of Akutagawa Ryūnosuke, a highly skilled writer with an encyclopedic knowledge of the Japanese language, poses many challenges for a translator. Multiple readings of any given poem are actively encouraged through his skillful use of the inherently enigmatic Japanese language, which, given its structure, depends heavily on wordplay, rhetorical devices, intuition, and suggestion. Any translation, then, simultaneously expands and reduces the possibilities of the original; indeed, a kind of translation even exists when read in Japanese, as haiku encourages active participation from the reader to in a sense complete a haiku by reading it.

In haiku particularly there exists an often intentional obscurity and terseness casually afforded by the language's structure, and haiku poets—particularly Akutagawa—frequently allude to other works of literature (Chinese poetry, Nō plays, etc.), and utilize *honkadori* (the direct quotation of lines and phrases from other poems). Great value is placed on what is said by what is not said, the comprehension of which depends upon a shared cultural heritage. Polysemous words, onomatopoeia, associations, double-entendres, *hibiki* (sonic or visual echoes), and *kakekotoba* (pivot words, homophones, word combinations, or other syntax used to create a variety of meanings) are frequently utilized, and the compression of these multiplications of meanings is the fundamental art of haiku.

It goes without saying that the Japanese language is vastly different from English. Most importantly, the two languages consist of widely divergent morphemes and sounds; rhythms, so important in Japanese poetry given its abundance of innate rhyme and its lack of stresses, involve *on*, time-based units in Japanese phonology, whereas English is syllabic and heavily stressed. Furthermore, in Japanese, there exist a plethora of non-translatable ellipses, enjambments, homonyms, pivot words, puns, slang, idioms, expressions, figures of speech, and dialects. Japanese is also abundantly polysemic and homonymic; an ideogrammatic language, it allows for visual resonances—as well as a visual aesthetic—that cannot possibly be replicated within the Latin alphabet. Moreover, unlike English,

Japanese lacks definite articles; makes no distinction between singular versus plural or masculine versus feminine—quantities and sexes must therefore be inferred—and lacks punctuation.

Significant cultural knowledge and linguistic attentiveness is required to interpret these subtle cues. Furthermore, certain words remain stubbornly untranslatable as there are no English equivalents. Japanese often expresses entirely unique concepts and ideas that remain totally and obstinately foreign to our understanding, and can therefore only be described in prose-like summary, thus completely negating the precision demanded by the haiku form.

What remains of the translator's considerably difficult work is hopefully elegant English language renderings of haiku that nevertheless must lose much of the poetic qualities available only in Japanese. Put plainly, to retain all of these meanings and effects— its art in Japanese, in other words—is more often than not hopelessly impossible if a translator means to still fashion them into some kind of harmonious poetic form. At best what can be retained from the originals is some of the gestative thought, gesture, and imagery.

Nevertheless, what is lost in translation arguably opens these haiku to certain, often unanticipated, gains. English, though a vastly different language from Japanese, does at least offer opportunities to explore a more linear version of the originals—mono versus stereo, if you will—with a vibrant music that only the English language can provide.

In these translations, I have aimed toward certain "verbal harmonies," to borrow translator Lenore Mayhew's now vintage yet still evocative description, and attempted to represent in English as best as possible the sound-sense of the originals. To replicate the 5-7-5 structure, never strictly adhered to in the original Japanese anyway, is foolish. Given the overall lack of polysyllabic words in English beyond, generally, two to three syllables, any attempt to match that structure results in overcrowding the verse with unnecessary words.

In spoken Japanese an *on* is more or less the same length. English accents cannot hope to replicate the syllabic uniformity of Japanese, which renders the 5-7-5 division absent accented and unaccented syllables unnatural for the English language. One benefit to the abandonment of this restriction is that the brevity and concision it affords in English is a serendipitous evocation of the very precise minimalism of the original.

As the title and subtitle indicate, the haiku in this collection are "versions" modeled *after* Akutagawa's haiku, interpretations and renditions of the originals, variations of Akutagawa's themes. Though these renderings are informed by a native Japanese speaker's input, given the inherent and intentional ambiguity of the haiku form, any potential for initial misreading—difficult to defend, given the semantic space and flexibility afforded by this ambiguity—is, in the spirit of haiku I think, explored rather than rejected.

Additional liberties were taken with the shape of the originals, given that English is, structurally, much different from Japanese; for example, Japanese has no relative pronouns and as a result, descriptive clauses are preceded by nouns. What's more, qualifying clauses precede nouns, and most haiku in Japanese end in verbs. Oftentimes, a strict adherence to word order results in clunky, awkward construction. As haiku nearly always dispenses with personal pronouns—rarely utilized in Japanese, anyway—I have resisted the use of pronouns where possible; occasionally, the construction of the English language demands their use for the purpose of clarification, and to wholly abandon pronouns often results in a forced, artificial construction, which for Western audiences detracts from the naturalness of the presentation. Image order is generally followed but in some cases abandoned entirely. Postpositions and kireji have no English equivalent and are mostly ignored. As for form, I generally follow the three-line rendering as introduced by R.H. Blyth, the creator of haiku in English, as that best seems to represent the original intent in Japanese. Only occasionally, haiku are rendered in two lines, but only where three-lines result in awkward construction.

The reader will notice that certain words are left

untranslated, and this is for a number of reasons: either the word is a proper name, has no satisfactory English equivalent or is in such common usage as to already be familiar to non-Japanese speakers (e.g., shōji, saké, etc.), or because sonically or rhythmically the Japanese fits better than a potential translation, at times all of the above. Where I have left a more obscure word or place name untranslated, I provide a note in the appendix.

In this present selection, I have included only those haiku in which I am most confident in my comprehension of the original, but where I have erred, or where subsequent information might correct or replace a prior *arrested* interpretation of that initial version is, in that rendering, superior, then a more accurate or correct translation—ultimately a misnomer, given the vast differences in the Japanese and English languages—is rejected. I have intentionally chosen to retain a perhaps not strictly slavish approximation of the original in the spirit of haiku that, again, invites a multiplicity of meanings as opposed to the decidedly unambiguous English in which they are presently rendered.

I nevertheless attempted to retain something of Akutagawa's classical diction, reflected in his frequent, eccentric use of archaic references and kanji.

The haiku are arranged seasonally, as opposed to chronologically. The original haiku, and their respective romaji renderings, are not included, as this collection is not an exercise in scholarship, but rather a creative work *inspired by*—as opposed to recreation from—Akutagawa's poetry.

赤内接
INSCRIBED RED

準えるの俳句バージョン芥川
Haiku Versions After Akutagawa Ryūnosuke

新年

first kimono of the year—
it is the same lonely feeling
of returning home

new year's day,
i venture out for the evening,
hands washed

new year's—
this evening
i tire of eating udon

春

winter lingers
in the mountains—
midnight

grass harvested
in the lingering winter
of the mountain depths

bamboo roots
within the earth
overcome the lingering cold

how many red turnips
were left behind?
winter lingers

crows and herons arrive
with the change of seasons—
we play go as winter lingers

winter lingers—
go played late
with rare stones

the skin of a conger eel
is drained—
winter lingers

on the trellis
pear tree buds appear green—
winter lingers

snow lingers
around a gravesite—
dragon's beard

seen within
the gaps of snow—
blue thorns

karatachi pruned—
spring snow

in the thaw
leaf blades hang—
yatsude

spring begins—
willow trellises
green

red spider lilies
rise up from the earth—
a damp wind

the scent
of a collapsed house—
thatched roof

thatched hut—
half of the pillar
is in spring sunlight

thatched hut—
spring sunlight
covers half the bridge

hung from the eaves
the wakame dries—
spring sunlight

early spring cold approaches—
a wakame wrapped package
unfastened

cold weather in early spring—
for medicine
a dose of wasabi

in the mountain behind the village
the sound of bamboo felled—
cold weather in early spring

cold weather in early spring—
among the bamboo groves
ginkaku-ji

so cold—
at midnight rain falls
on the neighbor's roof

rain falls
on the coolie's back—
red cross

clear, cold weather—
barefoot, a shellfish
stabs my sole

cold and clear—
branches fall
as a monkey descends

salamanders stirs
the cold waters
of early spring

fish eyes
poked with chopsticks—
clear and cold

cool, translucent fish heads
discarded
in the kitchen sink

new roads
always filled with stones—
cold spring weather approaches

gentle spring rain—
hinoki singed
with frost

hokosugi
scorched by frost
in springtime rain

snow thaws
in the middle of a field—
weeping willows droop

frost thaws—
bamboo yellows
by the roadside

frost turns to dew,
drains across the length
of yatsude

in thawed frost
stands the sentry
of dragon tongue orchids

a cluster of yellow trees
blossom at night—
water from melted snow

under the river of heaven
the sound of a swift current
intensifies

in gentle spring rain
a crane descends—
old beech leaves

wet from
gentle spring rain—
thin cuttings

gentle spring rain
everywhere among
the mountain snows

gentle spring rain
falls
on mountain snow

spring rain—
some snow still remains
on mount kai

silent southern temple—
lonesome
spring rain

gentle spring rain
and bamboo roots in rough dirt—
springtime

gentle spring rain—
withered bamboo grass
in a garden recess

in the garden
a small path
where azaleas bloom

garden lanterns
lined up in a row—
long incense sticks

the temple in spring
grows dark—
sotetsu's new leaves

short spring night—
steam blown from a cup of ginseng tea,
i drink

short spring night
grows dark—
i sink into the bath

sunlight pierces the sea
to the center
of the world

salt pan smoke
spreads across
the spring sea

smoke from shiogama
drifts out
across the springtime sea

distant mist at sea—
people eat
on a small island

legend has it that
xu fu departed ages ago—
midday sea grows misty

on a mountain cliff
the water trickles—
mists increase

pine tree resin dribbles
when misty mountains fill
with blossoming buds

clouds? mountains?
the sun in a misty haze—
biwa waterfall

water that drips
from the mountain cliffs—
it too is misty

keenly cold—
a pear tree buds
in spring rain

a white peach
moistened,
a red peach smoked

white peach—
buds wet,
branches bend

lilies sprout in the green
along the embankment—
sun's shadow in dried grass

on the mountain
cedar fires burn—
only the echoes are clear

mountain fire—
a clear echo
among the cedars

airplanes travel east
to kyoto—
morning clouds

uguisu under the eaves
dry off in the heat—
fires on the scree

white magnolia—
a sparrow swallows
its voice

in the lower leaves
of a tōjuro tree
a sparrow pauses

sanmon gate
at night—
a kite faintly sings

uguisu and akane—
of little significance
to mountain trees

march—
useless akane
used as thatching

uguisu—
a bit of akane
among mountain timber

evening drifts away—
uguisu
beneath the eaves

the danger of the cranes
crossing over the stones—
spring torrents

evening cold water ablutions—
stones wet by the petals
of hanging wisteria

six purple wisteria flowers
six feet long
offered in worship of the buddha

late afternoon
cuttlefish grilled—
wisteria blossoms

in the afternoon
dried squid roasted—
wisteria blossom

wisteria blossoms
in the eaves—
moss grows old

wisteria blossoms—
moss deteriorates
on the eaves

wisteria blossoms—
the sun shines
on the other side of nara

white plums blossoms—
the roof of shōren'in
concealed by clouds

piled atop the cow—
goryō of hinoki cypress
and apricot blossoms

apricot seeds
divided between
two or three people

afflicted with fever,
shivering in
cherry blossom light

thatched hut—
a mirror reflects
the plum blossoms

if you look closely—
tree sparrow trapped
in a thatched roof

idle sunday
at play
among plum blossoms

pear blossoms
appear cold—
a palanquin rushes by

people come and go
among pear blossoms—
darkness approaches the village

the sweet fragrance
of the blossoms—
misty moon

peach blossoms
and smoke shadows
in the pasture

peach blossoms—
the mud turtle
has slept all day

rape blossoms grow
untouched by mud
in the rain

rape blossoms grow
without becoming dirty
in the rain

the sound of the ocean—
in the long valley
rape blossoms and dame's rocket

late cherry blossoms—
eggs cracked,
left to rot

my inn,
ankoromochi—
blossoms fall

blossoms fall—
the ox's forehead
becomes dusty

blossoms scatter—
set foot upon
the withered ground

mountain blossoms scatter—
a mother and child together
relax beside the chrysanthemum pond

flowers fall—
the thermometer
grows silent

yellow flowers
in the rain
bow to the ground

rice boiled over a fire
at the rice field's edge—
plum tree blossom

even under
the state's dictatorship
ume blooms

still in bloom
under the eaves—
flowers and tea smoke

here and there
among the countryside,
flowers and tea smoke

tea plantation
in the setting sun—
a place to stay

tea field in sunlight
continues—
my home village

near my home
flowers bloom—
so too does the coarse tea

dark grotto—
yatsude seeds
scattered in spring

spring wind blows
through copious new leaves—
higashiyama

spring wind
blows through the cedars
of a lonely mountain village

tips of wheat in sunlit spring wind—
enlightenment in the soot
of a forest grove

on the roadside
rows of wheat ears grow red—
springtime

wind in spring sun—
ears of wheat
and clouds of soot

the soot from shinonome
falls down inside
shimonoseke

in the middle of the night
the charcoal fire
dimly lit

late at night
illuminated by firelight
the faces of the infant chicks

spring moon
in the evergreen trees—
the water's edge grows faint

in a saloon by the sea,
an evergreen tree
grows from a bowl

dark melancholy—
spring morning sun
shines on black pines

spring day—
dew dangles
from bamboo branches

spring day—
bamboo branches sag
from the weight of water

spring breeze
in the bamboo grass—
footprints vanished

scissors
catch the nail—
early spring

cold weather floats
over the cistern—
evening falls

the bodhisattva's name
is xīn wáng—
spring winds

spring breeze—
in bamboo grass the foot of the mountain
disappears

stepladder used to prune
a crowded box wood tree—
spring breeze

spring breeze
blows down
young birds

bees chew
clumps of earth—
spring breeze

returned home
to my grass hut—
spring breeze

spring breeze—
the clear blue eyes
of a young bride

dropped from the second floor
an ornate hairpin—
cold and clear

polka dot hairpin—
a cool spring breeze
combs her hair

island-style ornate hairpin
made from seashells—
spring breeze

shirozake and shōji—
a gentle breeze
and cloudy weather

shōji closed,
the high wind dies down—
sakuramochi

gramophone sound stops—
before one's eyes
an antique yoshido

eyelashes trimmed,
examined—
spring sunset

the sea and the sky over edo—
spring weather
becomes hazy

hazy spring weather—
no regrets letting go
of an old love

hazy spring weather—
old love abandoned
without regret

stone slime—
sadness
in water's sunlight

vines spread
into the bright
spring water

morning glories—
in wet dirt
bamboo vines creep

morning glory vines
overflow
the flowerpots

cherry trees
in the light of dawn
reach the third floor

old man's shadow
and a cat swallowed
by a pool of water

disease of the bladder,
confined within
a resplendent room

the medal's weight—
an aged body's
first light

light—
in cloudy water
a dead man's fingers stir

a red-faced bureaucrat
receives a wooden statue
wrapped in tinfoil

warm pistils
painted with wax—
tsukuribana

daytime—
a trembling star gently shines
in the mist

a row of white willows
by the roadside
shrouded in mist

beside the swamp
a row of trees
in a hazy mist

kite triangle
square hexagon
sky glass

hot springs—
the bottom of the jar
is smooth

the electric sign
above the grass door—
kiji in the canopy

upstream—
peaches smoked
in a thatched hut village

from a pipe
peach smoke billows
and water leaks

kudzu stirred with chopsticks,
i flinch—
spring evening

light clouds
gather in parsley—
unstirred

in the garden,
mayflies grow intimate
with satsuki

may rains—
bitter chestnuts float
on the water's surface

may rains—
market cabbage
passes into darkness

may rains fall
on a wall
of namako

nowadays
absorbed in writing trifles—
hazy spring weather

hazy water—
fallen petals
float

heat haze
obscures
white butterflies

onsen hu's
smooth base—
a long spring day

sunset lengthens
in late spring—
even the monks feel lonely

in the temple,
springtime ends—
sago's young leaves

夏

early summer rain—
round loquat dwells
in a grove

early summer rain—
in the river stream
something wrapped in a bamboo mat

early summer rain—
people buy tamana
in darkness

early summer rain—
brushwood stacked
under the eaves

eight yen bento
to go—
early summer breeze

red roots—
early afternoon,
fresh leaves bend the trees

peach tree
covered by a blanket of flowers—
branches bend

in garden grass
the light haze of heat
at summer's start

bamboo shoot's skin—
light heat at the start of summer
flows

bamboo shoots
grow red—
summer equinox

rare butterfly
in the distance—
a simple brilliance

at my bedside
anna karenina—
flower blossoms

tanabata—
evening flower blossoms
and the roar of the sea

on a rope
white shirts hung to dry—
paulownia blossom

the sun
on the flower's waxy pistil—
drops of dew

wisteria blossoms
heavy with rain
for a fleeting moment

thatched roof—
lilies bloom
around a small and simple home

when the day lilies bloom
it's time to say goodbye

evening moon—
fragrances cling
to the blossom

hayagruva seen
for the very first time—
shinji rape flowers

tree peonies cut,
my heart lifts
into the sky

tree peonies cut—
the heart ascends to see
the evening clouds

overwhelmed
by cloudy weather,
tree peonies bloom

ant lion hides
inside the red
tree peony blossom

the sound of footsteps
approaching over
fallen tree peonies

from the bonbai branch
the plum's mustache
hangs

clouds fade
from a bathhouse window—
melon blossoms

flowers strung
from an iron wire—
open window

stateroom window linen—
i write
in the setting sun

an american
bangs wildly
at a typewriter

jiji shinpō office—
world map tacked to the wall
slowly darkens

at dusk,
surrounded by mysteries—
electric fan

samurai's bamboo screen
lowers—
crape myrtle

on the opposite side
of a green bamboo screen
flowers grow in a secluded garden

geta placed
right beside me—
irises

breeze from a river—
wise irises
tell fortunes

new rainbow—
blue irises
on the roof

rainbow in the east—
the sun in its place
over tokyo

distant clouds—
poppy flowers intermingle
with waves of grain

red poppies—
every night, every night,
simplicity opens

ah, the silence—
summer camellias
wildly scattered

floating weeds—
destination unknown
but for love

ancient gold-refining kiln—
kakuidori

the sun's shadows fade
into a mulberry bush—
noon bell chimes

hototogisu plucks
mountain mulberries
in morning heat

wide field—
white shoes a sheath
for hototogisu

weeds mown down—
bell flowers and
hototogisu

hay dangles
from bamboo rakes—
hototogisu

morning glow approaches
the sky over biwa—
hototogisu

hototogisu—
walls painted
with algae

the morning after
guangshi ignores
the hototogisu

a voice cries
and rain falls—
hototogisu

thin light curtain
illuminated by a single candle—
saké cup and hototogisu

morning star—
chirori echoes
a distant hototogisu

on red curtains
gold letters
billow smoke

for the bats
a flame is thin silk—
rashōmon

bats—
blue paper lanterns hang
from moonlit willow trees

bats—
the mortician works
in canal water's light

bat country—
cherry trees
full of mold

a flock of summer butterflies
hovers above
a pile of shit

summer butterflies' wings
come to a sudden stop—
horseshit

blazing heat—
a butterfly stops to rest
in horseshit

from his throne
the river cicada watches
a small boat pass

outside the gate
a deep pool and several trees—
sudden chorus of cicadas

in a vacant garden
a lone cicada sings—
moonlight

the sound of cicadas
throughout the night
lit by a thin moon

pregnant female snake
at rest in the rain—
silk tree blossom

abandoned
in a hot water bath—
a frog to kill

mountain stream
shallows at dawn—
kajika frog

is the green tree frog
freshly painted
also?

dry umbrellas
folded separately—
evening frogs

dull weather—
a frog lives
inside of a jar

dull weather—
a pit viper lives
inside of a jar

sawagani breath
bubbles up
then disappears

in clear water
big fish
come and go

river stream hunting—
in the porcelain brightness of a deep pool
tao ch'ien tucks up the hem of his garments

in silence
a master works—
the rainy season begins

shirohae—
a high wave
roars

a dolphin pod migrates,
whistles and clicks—
rainy season sea

southerly wind over open sea
at the start of the rainy season—
clicks and whistles of migratory dolphins

white south wind—
the sound of dolphins
heard across the big river

white south wind
above the open sea—
a pod of dolphins sing

white south wind
high evening waves
roar

the south wind
shakes the sea
at dawn

the open ocean
flattened
by the black south wind

in the sky
an evening shower approaches—
lotus flowers

dry grass
and lotus flowers
soaked with rain

cattail tip
lightly sways
a lotus flower

dreams—
cool white lotus
sways above my pillow

tile-colored rock at dusk—
lotuses
here and there

moonless dawn—
a whitefish plays
with the sacred lotus

from the lotuses
in morning darkness
a whitefish springs

a multitude
of exotic women—
lotus blossoms

a mountain rain approaches
and all the lotus flowers
bow down

chimaki unwrapped,
xuanzong presented
to the high priest

sole of feet seen—
buddhist priest's nap

covered
in wheat dust—
a child sleeps

wheat dust
covers the child—
still asleep

the wheat harvester
is tired—
daytime moon

a coachman
and his white horses rest idle
in a field of wheat

the wheat
has gone to waste
in the darkness

sunset dyed
the color
of wild wheat

hashitaka flies
across a wide field
of wheat

a horse rests
in the bamboo grass
of the outer citadel

sun and horses
completely obscured
by bamboo grass

the scent of bamboo grass
in a field—
the sun at its apex

garden lawn—
a path cuts through
the azalea blossoms

sasahara and sasa
stand as tall
as the horizon

flower lily—
neighbor's envy
pierces the bamboo screen

majestic houses
crowded together—
evening silk tree blossoms

night falls
on the cloisonné pillars—
evening silk tree blossoms

golden buddha's hands
clasped in prayer—
silk tree blossoms

evening moon—
pagoda trees blended
with silk tree flowers

the loneliness
of a lama temple—
silk tree blossoms

darkness approaches
the brass rings
of a buddhist temple gate

temples
are merely wood and stone—
evening cold

swastika column—
fish dried
under a blue sky

evening glow—
fog creeps in across the sun
and the soft rushes of the rice field waters

summer mountain—
layers of lingering evening light
accumulate

summer mountains
seem empty
in the lingering light of evening

summer mountain—
pine tree colors
drained by storm clouds

summer mountain and sky
dimly lit—
dark storm clouds

summer mountain—
leaves rise
in tempest clouds

embarked on a trip
from makuwa,
sweet months of leisure

after crossing several valleys
we reach this place—
hitorimushi

rain falls heavy
upon the castle town—
nihohi

does the day grow late?
on the branches
leaves luxuriate

hatsuma hokora
lamplit in rain

wind and rain
pass through
green paddies

wind summoned
by the paddy field's soft rushes—
morning clouds

stone elephant's belly—
warm summer moon

large elephants
wear hanagasa—
festival

hanagusa
decorated with peonies
at the festival

green reeds and a rainbow—
house on the outskirts,
five or six feet

white plaster walls and
bashō rolled into a ball—
nankin-ji

tōji temple—
bashō rolls
fatten

banana peeled
under a cool summer moon—
skin discarded

this dim sum
is inadequate yet
the tea is fresh

awake late at night—
loach soup
grows lukewarm

kudzu water in a cup
measured out
with a spoon

evening shower—
the dirt floor
covered with mantō

evening shower—
ginkgo leaves
near the castle gate

after a bath,
niwageta lit
by summer moon

umbrellas
in moonlight—
two people

your parasol
darkens
into purple simplicity

fallen sick by the wayside
in the scorching sun—
flies swarm

under the blazing sun
frenzied people
and no clouds

in red glow,
a gun carriage drawn—
horse's sweat

twilight
and a lightning bug
come to kill

mosquito net
catches the eye
in morning light

the blazing sun ascends—
winnow dust
never disappears

scorching sun
burns up the dust
from the winnow basket

in the blazing sun
thunder from
the roots of a tree

red lily pistils
blacken
in the extreme heat

scorching sun—
lizard's tail even if severed
stirs

a butterfly's tongue
is a flowering fern
in summer heat

butterfly's tongue
like a royal fern
resembles the heat of spring

a small rabbit droops
a single ear
in the blistering heat

on a tiled roof
and carpet
lie dried insects

tree branch
touches
tile hotness

the north wind blows
yet in tokyo
the sun still burns

summer mountain sky—
the small darkness
of approaching storm clouds

summer mountains—
lightning strikes
a single place

under the midday sun
mountain trees
dissolve

a multi-flora rose
reaches its peak

soot from a variety of leaves
drifts
into the long summer night

smoke from a cigar
drifts in an unbroken stream
into the long summer night

sunflowers grow
loud and lurid
at one o'clock

sunflower blossoms
brighten
in the heat

bit by bit
sunflowers wither
in midsummer heat

sunflowers slowly
wither away
in late summer heat

the heat
from dokudama blossoms
fills the entire rack

evening heat—
into the rice fields descends
countless wild geese

short summer night—
into evergreen magnolia blossoms
a crane dives

mountain wind
blows a heron down
into the paddy field

wind blows down
an empty road
lined with flax

at midday
overgrown boughs
bend down

fallen plums
scattered in a field
of green onions

summer onions
in dark earth
desiccate

harvested wheat
spills over
into the strawberries

sunshine—
resin scent
in the pine forest

banana peeled
under a cool summer moon—
skin discarded

cold weather
at twilight—
ocean waters

path surrounded
by a bamboo forest—
the night is cold

crude drawing—
shades of a mountain
blanketed in mist

moss carpets
the crape myrtle—
autumn approaches

秋

first day of autumn—
my tooth filled
with silver

autumn begins—
mount kongō
is cloudless

autumn mist
swaddles
the akane

autumn—
the akane no longer wears
its infant clothes

early autumn rain—
a layer of darkness approaches
the twelfth floor

early autumn—
morning glories open
in late afternoon

a locust caught
in early autumn

senyaku smoke
stirs up
the crickets

daybreak—
in the rafters
crickets quieten

from inside an ash gourd
a cricket crawls—
early morning

shoes polished
in the mist—
second bloom

dried flower blossoms
scattered on the lawn
trampled over

rough bamboo screen—
beneath, ignoring the rain,
a small round snail

hidden
in autumn barley—
strawberries

morning dew
on mountain ivy
drips down its many leaves

dew forms
on blackened fruit—
a swarm of birds

vines moisten—
crow gourd

in a basket
glistens
a hot plum

from a boulder
water drips—
crescent moon

crescent moon—
white figs
ripen early

river of heaven—
eggplant seeds
accumulate

goat hair sheared—
cleared
autumn pastures

two pines trees
withered by a flood—
red spider lily

two pine trees
among village pampas grass—
red spider lily

the sound of wind in the pines
and crimson chōchin—
autumn scream

wind blows through the pines—
the fire has not exterminated
a single person

cotton roses here and there—
changdeokgung shrine
on a moonlit night

autumn wind
dries the wet
cotton thread

scattered
in the autumn breeze
the ash of bones

autumn breeze—
from a dark mole grows
a single hair

worn wood
of the pepper tree
still stands against the autumn wind

autumn wind—
measured on a scale
the carp's length

eating grapes—
a song made
of autumn wind

fragrant olives—
in the evening
stone steps grow damp

sandalwood fruit
heard in the breeze—
stone steps

wind blows
through the pines—
visiting a grave

the thought of home
sickens me—
hot autumn

body feverish,
drowsily nodding off—
a long night

autumn—
inside a mosquito net
an invalid coughs

bai zhi—
a new dose of medicine
this autumn morning

autumn—
upon waking,
an invalid coughs

alone
early in the morning—
mountain bellflower

autumn bellflower—
winds increase
in the evening sky

wind dies,
clouds part—
stars appear

downtown
darkened by cloudy skies—
night full of stars

everyone can see
the clouds rise—
starry night

the color
of thin clouds—
starry night

starry night
above the mountain range—
a low growl

at daybreak
birds clamor
in an autumn shower

exposed to the sun
millet unravels
in the field

millet and radish
wither in
daytime sunlight

a white duck
rests against
the dry stone wall

the call of wild geese—
paper lanterns hang
in a millet field

setting sun—
over the millet field
wild geese fly

the cries of the wild geese
fall—
potato leaves rustle

pampas grass trimmed
along a wide hill—
wild geese migrate

the sound of wild geese—
in the eaves
dried peppermint

wild geese
and yellowed grass—
burial mound

wild geese dive
and sing as they fall—
night arrives

the moon rises
and the wild geese fall—
tsukadajima

above my hermitage
flying past the moon—
the call of the wild geese

in the shape
of one hundred wild geese
the moon rises

a trace of the moon
in the descent
of a wild goose

the moon wanes—
upside down
a wild goose descends

crescent moon—
a single wild goose
descends

rainy night in asakusa—
lamplight and
a flock of wild geese

a flock of wild geese
descends from the sky—
daytime fireworks

clearly seen
far offshore—
distant fireworks

jinriksha moves
through darkness—
fireworks

water darkens,
fireworks cease—
evening jinriksha

fireworks fall,
water stirs—
all is still

autumn—
blown by the wind,
afternoon fireworks extinguished

evening light—
seen from the fire lookout,
distant fireworks

In imitation of Hiroshigé

seen from the watchtower,
distant fireworks
illuminate the night

crimson hour—
from under the eaves
an itoki's song ends

mild autumn day—
eagle owl roosts
on a bamboo branch

autumn day—
the enoki tree
leans toward the ground

rain at sunset—
in the eaves
sponge gourd and nashi

sunset—
when the plowing stops
the ocean can be heard

blue sea roar
in late afternoon
recedes

the sun goes down
and the ploughing stops—
the sound of the ocean

in starlight
sailors still look up—
sextant

wood and stone
in the eaves—
night draws near

among the bamboo
the sound of a temple flute—
plum pine forest

autumn sun—
bamboo hangs from a hedge
like shide

morning glory ivy
tangled within
the bamboo vine

lacquer tree ivy
crawls through the cold garden
pine trees

bamboo
autumn shrine—
the torii can't be seen

autumn ink painting—
in broad daylight
bamboo in view

clear autumn sky—
in the bathroom window
two bamboo

a single pole
of meng bamboo—
autumn stirs

hatsuma—
hokora lamp extinguished
in the rain

tea house on the canal
battered by rain—
a single guest

suzukake—
coffee shop beneath
the flower blossoms

beneath
the suzukake blossom—
a coffee shop

roasted barley flour
stirred into boiled water—
autumn

some autumns...
the color of saké
in antique cups

chrysanthemum saké ladled—
the white robes
of wang wei

first awase kimono of the year—
gold for the second-born
imperial prince

wind heard
in the pines—
old kimono

sword prohibition removed—
just as before,
my yellow kimono

the presented sword
tested this morning—
autumn

the scent of leather
and foreign imported books
in clear autumn weather

high spirits—
yuzumiso sits silent
on the small low table

edamame served—
fan varnished with
persimmon juice

mountain shrouded
in low red clouds—
persimmon leaves

in a thatched hut
eleven persimmons
are an evening's abundance

the sound of the ocean—
autumn sun sets
over the millet field

on the lacquer tray
autumn accompanies
the shells of a crab

autumn breeze—
leftover crab shells
on a tray

autumn saba... ah!
salted and dried
an entire day

distant sands—
above the tips of grass
sea clouds

parasol held—
there is a strange beauty to
kanji in the sand

over the sea
the autumn sun sets—
cane field

on the mast,
a lapis lazuli lamp hangs—
autumn ocean

xing qiu—
darkness appears
inside the garden

giyaman garden
lanterns lit—
autumn ocean

village grasshoppers
make good use
of garden lanterns

light rain—
leftover chinese lanterns
on the grass

light rain falls
over an old home
in the mountains

each of the withered leaves
on the paulownia tree
is unique

incense burned
and then the first autumn leaf
falls

kirishitanzaka—
the "hill of the christians"—
suddenly grows cold

moon in the mountains
shines brightly—
the scent of fallen leaves

in the cloudy twilight,
bits of wood and leaves
used for kindling

furnace ashes spill—
tree leaves
used as kindling

autumn sun—
on the enoki tips
leaves flutter

a bundle of incense sticks—
the first fallen leaves
of autumn

incense recedes
and then falls
the first leaves of autumn

in the mountains
a clear moon and
the scent of fallen leaves

joy felt
from the fallen leaves
at rest beneath a hazy moon

at night—
fallen leaves burned
to protect a kami

among evening autumn leaves
i weep—
rimless tin chaki

sanmon—
a monk in purple robes
steps on fallen leaves

fallen leaves of the ginkgo tree
fallen leaves of the cherry trees—
leaving home

at the bottom
of a sumitori
faint leaves

mountain moon
bright and clear—
the scent of fallen leaves

burning
the pitiable remains
of fallen leaves

intently,
a small child crawls to her mother—
sasachimaki

an infant coughs—
damp with sweat
on a chilly night

only child's zōri dried—
stems and leaves
of harvested rice

a child's zōri
left to dry—
this year's straw

even the charcoal fire
breathes—
evening twilight

the apparition in evening twilight
of a doll clothed
in chrysanthemum flowers

the demon-like eyelashes
cause discomfort—
doll clothed in chrysanthemum flowers

suspiciousness—
twilight approaches
a doll clothed in chrysanthemum flowers

white chrysanthemums—
fragrance also
in their shade and light

with reluctance,
a white chrysanthemum falls—
autumn rain

autumn rain—
where the tree is planted
the color of the soil

autumn storm—
in the daigokuden
rain leaks

lightning strike—
silence
of the north star

lightning bolt—
ayakashi appears
in the ship's sails

bamboo garden
grounds swept—
late autumn storm

late autumn storm—
wind howls in the thatched roof
of the hermitage

wintersweet—
among its sparse branches
late autumn rain begins to fall

wintersweet—
scattered branches
in late autumn rain

white chrysanthemums
in late autumn rain
decay

grey starling
struck by pebbles—
late autumn storm

late autumn storm ends—
a single insect
begins to sing

late autumn day—
tree sparrows nest
in the village

late autumn day—
an owl nests motionless
in bamboo branches

late autumn day ends—
shadows
on an antique shōji

sunset on this late autumn day
arrives too soon—
old shōji

the voice of the evening bird
grows silent—
late autumn

the red of the crow gourd
deepens—
late autumn rainstorm

where did seigetsu
leave his gourd?
late autumn

a woman's name
written in the ashes
of the hibachi

if you look at me
even my fine clothes
grow cold

first frost of autumn—
kumquat
among dense leaves

morning chill—
leaf blades dangle
from daimyo oak

morning chill—
white ripples appear
on the river's surface

morning chill—
ground cherries spill
into the weeds

fallen chestnuts—
on a distant mountain path
moonlight approaches

another evening approaches—
loach soup
becomes lukewarm

lying down
on a long autumn night—
tatami scent

autumn sun—
tatami dried
on the other side of town

the mountains of hachidō
stand bald—
autumn morning

in the storm's mist
mountain folds
grown dim

mountain ravine—
among the cedars
a clear echo

in the perfect circle
of the setting sun
a path lined with cedars

bamboo thicket
on a cold night
at a crossroads

light reflected
in the mud—
cold night

tea loses its color—
on a cold night
alone

cold night—
on the neighbor's roof
what remains of the moon after midnight

trees and stones
lie down in a garden—
cold night

garden trees and stones
reflect
the evening cold

autumn cools—
moss clings
to every branch

what moss remains
on garden stones—
late autumn

my friend pisses
on a black cobblestone
in sparse grass

alone at night beside the ancestral tomb
composing ki—
coldness

hyōnō—
the sound of loose
autumn ice

weeping willow—
its tears
are fallen snow

冬

early winter rain
falls where i live—
radishes left to dry in the sun

at night a yuzu falls
onto the bright earth—
early winter rain

early winter rain—
at the canal tea house
a single visitor

early winter rain—
daybreak at the summit
of higashiyama

facing the center of the ravine
two hayagriva—
first winter rain

in early winter rain
a dog approaches—
a sack for charcoal

the charcoal's charred remains
continue to burn
late into the winter night

first frost—
the mind resides
inside a grove

first frost—
a kumquat fallen
among the leaves

blue kutsu
left behind—
goryeo frost

frost at nightfall—
sugegasa
come and go

thin cotton stretched
to match the kimono's length—
frosty evening

frost forms
across
a bamboo hat

winter frost—
to be mindful
today and tomorrow

the sound of cedars
frozen deep
in the ravine

low to the horizon
the sound of cedars
freezing

twilight sky—
frozen cedar trees
deathly still

dark sky—
the sound of cedar trees
frozen over

old bones
concealed inside
leather haori

morning chill—
I lie down,
the sound of a straw blanket

cold winter wind—
belly full
of medicine

hospital room tray—
morning chill,
raw egg

a short time to roast—
the crab lies bright
on the mantis shrimp platter

midnight coal fire
weakens—
meat boiled down

extreme cold—
yōkan remains
at the bottom of the dish

painful cough—
beautiful cheek seen
beneath a winter hat

kurozoka—
my hair
a knitted snow boshi

listening to the sound
of wind in the pines—
straw hat

cold wintry wind—
in cogon grass
the sound of kasa

yamamoto—
kasa pass into
the frosty night

long night
at the mountain's base—
kasa pass by

cold wintry wind—
bai zhi wrapped
in a small white cloth

lake teganuma—
duck bestowed
with coldness

cape wetlands at midday—
the stillness
of withered grass

wind blows
across the withered grass—
winter shadow

wind blows
through a withered grove—
winter shadows

what is it that stirs
on the temple's pole?
a flag or the winter wind?

cold winter wind—
the sun is far
from tokyo

cold winter wind—
tree roots bound
to a rocky mountain

cold winter wind—
dried sardines retain
the color of the sea

evening waves—
oysters in the belly
of an old ship

profound sorrow—
the brightness
of the sea

slowly the clouds approach
a withered inn—
teri kumori

withered thicket—
charcoal fire kindled by the wind
awakens the home

a wife applies
her first erioshiroi—
midwinter evening approaches

white plum blossoms—
midwinter evening rain approaches
the samurai town

the knife is cold
and midwinter cloudy—
the chives are cut

cleaning up, building a fire,
midwinter mountain—
fallen leaves swept away

arhat's ribs
deepen
in midwinter cold

morning—
bed head and midwinter
teeth creak

even the ruts in the road
are deep in thicket shadow—
winter sun

the grove shadows reach further
into the furrows—
winter sun

tea smoke
flutters from my room—
higashiyama

idle chatter—
flames extinguished
by fire alarms

many shadows on the sands
of a dry riverbed—
december

the many shadows of december
cover even the recesses
of dry riverbed sands

deep roots
of the trees—
mountain shadows

in a hedge
sasanqua mingles
with shadows

sasanqua leaves
intertwined within a hedge—
the shadow of a cloud

for a sasanqua flower,
the young geisha names a high price—
winter cold

her soft belly
rises and falls—
a prostitute asleep at noon

negi-like,
the long white fingers
of a streetwalker

the sound of setta
in bamboo grass—
masajirō kojima

withered grass—
across the garden
a row of stones

stepping stones
laid diagonally
through the withered grass

inside the gate
a long line of paving stones
grow cold

the sound of wind in the pines—
withered grass
on a solitary peak

winter sky—
sound of the second floor
swept out

bamboo cut
through its center—
midwinter morning sun rises

bamboo grove
low in a ravine—
the wind approaches rapidly

winter sun—
shōji shadows
on bamboo screens

winter sun—
on the shōji
bamboo shadows

winter sun—
imposed on the shōji
bamboo shadows

snow in bamboo
at sunset—
valley stream

at dusk
snow flutters down
into bamboo

in front of the bamboo thicket
a ball of snow
bathed in sunlight

happy to peel
broiled sweet chestnuts—
snowy night

light snow inside
a garden courtyard—
oranges on the hedge

in my garden
snow is sewn
to every tree branch

twigs gathered—
someone's piled them up
in the snow

snow falls
and accumulates into drifts—
evening

sliding down
the withered glass—
room's blossom

mountainous country—
shijimi to reach
next spring

the color of the hydrangeas
brings such peace—
even so

impromptu

1

someone plays
with a broken piece of jade—
hototogisu

the whiteness of my fingers
observed—
hototogisu

a single silk curtain, a saké cup,
a lamp lit in one a.m. rain—
hototogisu

2

spring has settled
in the mountains,
suikazura in the shade

a clump of wood shavings
and yellow flowers
in a puddle of melted snow

ERIC HOFFMAN recently translated Sumitaku
Kenshin's *Unfinished*, published by Spuyten
Duyvil. A poet, essayist, and editor, he lives
and works in Connecticut.